T5-CCJ-775

CRISISPOINTS FOR WOMEN

Where Is God When I Need Him Most?

by Janet Kobobel

A MINISTRY OF THE NAVIGATORS
P.O. BOX 35001, COLORADO SPRINGS, COLORADO 80935

The Navigators is an international Christian organization. Jesus Christ gave His followers the Great Commission to go and make disciples (Matthew 28:19). The aim of The Navigators is to help fulfill that commission by multiplying laborers for Christ in every nation.

NavPress is the publishing ministry of The Navigators. NavPress publications are tools to help Christians grow. Although publications alone cannot make disciples or change lives, they can help believers learn biblical discipleship, and apply what they learn to their lives and ministries.

ISBN 08910-96507

Cover illustration by Greg Hally.

CRISISPOINTS FOR WOMEN series edited by Judith Couchman.

This series offers God's hope and healing for life's challenges.

All Scripture quotations in this publication are from the *Holy Bible: New International Version* (NIV). Copyright © 1973, 1978, 1984, International Bible Society. Used by permission of Zondervan Bible Publishers.

Printed in the United States of America

C O N T E N T S

Introduction: Has God Disappeared?   7
Then this study guide could help you find Him.

Crisispoint: When God Seems Silent   9
What you need to know when you feel abandoned.

Evaluation: Lose Your Security Lately?   23
Assess how you respond to a painful crisis.

Bible Lessons:

  1 Expect the Unexpected   27
     God's ways may puzzle and surprise you.

  2 Of Guarantees and Warranties   37
     God doesn't promise to always rescue you.

  3 Lookin' Good Ain't Enough   49
     Develop a healthy heart in a sick situation.

  4 Who Me, Mad?   59
     When God does something you don't like.

  5 The Quintessential Sufferer   71
     Job's example can help you find rest.

Dialogue: Making Sense of Suffering   87
Questions for group or individual reflection.

Bibliography: Making More Sense   93
Suggested readings to console and encourage.

To Rita and Debbie,
who suffered through the writing with me.

ACKNOWLEDGMENTS

Bouquets of thanks to Sheila Cragg for lending me her library and to Larry Weeden and Marjorie Kurz for their moral support.

A special bouquet to Judith Couchman for providing me the chance to use my painful past experiences to benefit others; for her words of encouragement; and most importantly, for the fragrance of her friendship. ■

Has God Disappeared?

*Then this study guide could help
you find Him.*

Pam believed that God answered prayer. So
she prayed every day on her knees, when she
realized her marriage was floundering.

But prayer didn't save her marriage.
Instead, the heavens seemed constructed of
lead, keeping her requests from permeating
to her Helper. And Pam wondered why God
chose not to respond to her pleas.

When you're in desperate straits, the last
thing you want from God is silence. "Silence
is the worst form of persecution," said Blaise
Pascal, a seventeenth-century religious
writer.[1] And who could devastate us more
with silence than God?

If you've struggled over God's silence
when you're desperately calling Him; if
you've been angry or hurt by unanswered
prayer; then this study guide could be a
stimulus for your perplexed faith.

Not that this booklet contains simple steps for getting God to respond. Not that it will take away emotional pain. But it could help you admit that God has been unresponsive or downright disappointing in meeting your needs. Squarely facing this truth is the beginning of a deeper, richer relationship with Him.

This study guide will help you understand common responses to emotional or physical pain. And where to look for God when you feel He doesn't care. You'll also examine who God is. Because when you lose sight of His inimitable qualities, His silence becomes deeply disturbing.

But I warn you: Some of His ways are full of surprise. A friend once announced to me, "God is silly." Far from a sacrilegious thought, I've discovered it to be accurate. God's ways can be full of mystery, irony, and from our perspective, absurdity.

This booklet's self-assessment section will also help you understand how you respond during His silent times. And five Bible lessons and group questions will help redirect you down more productive, faith-filled paths.

Above all, you'll grapple with the question, "Where is God when I need Him most?" The answer can bring comfort midst the pain of your circumstances. ∎

—JANET KOBOBEL

NOTE
1. Blaise Pascal, *The Penses* (New York: French and European Publications, 1962), page 36.

When God Seems Silent

What you need to know when you feel abandoned.

Patti stood at the side of the hospital bed, studying her husband's battered, swollen face. Tubes protruded from the man she loved, connecting him to machines that gurgled and pumped as they surrounded his bed. She nervously worked a crease into the sheet, its startling crispness seeming more real to her than anything else in the room.

She recalled how, earlier that evening, she started to wave goodbye to James as he left for an evening jog. But she called him back, insisting he wear his jacket with the reflectors. *Had she guessed something unspeakable might happen?*

Hours later, when James hadn't returned, Patti called the police to report him missing. Eventually she learned that, during his run along a busy highway, he zagged on to the road and a car hit him.

The impact flung him into the oncoming traffic, and another car ran over him. Now he lay in a coma.

Patti took his hand and squeezed it. She bent down and whispered into his ear a prayer and a demand. "God, restore James's health. Tomorrow morning, let him wake up and be himself again," she cried.

But thirty-three-year-old James didn't wake up the next morning, or the next, or the next. Six months later, after James lost fifty pounds and his limbs curved into unnatural curlicues, he quietly slipped away.

During those months, Patti had prayed fervently, believing God would answer—believing He had to answer. As James drifted closer to death every day, Patti remained steadfast in her faith. She believed God would move on their behalf, showing Himself strong and capable of the miraculous.

When the end came, the beginning of a terrible season started for Patti. In some ways, it felt worse than the months of James's coma. Patti had lost not only her husband, but also her God.

DEEPEST NEED

Some of us have suffered major losses, as Patti did. Others of us don't know that kind of pain. But it doesn't lessen our longing to hear from God in our moments of deepest need. Times of suffering, whether physical or emotional, increase our urgency to know that

10

God hears us, that He is aware of our suffering, that He is with us.

During emergencies, we can experience an awful sense of abandonment. That's because we're afraid of losing the "temples" in our lives. Temples are the earthly things we depend on for security. And since they're physical rather than spiritual, these temples are fragile instead of firm. They include our loved ones, marriage, children, economic support, and physical well-being.

When any of these temples collapses, we may respond in different ways.

Rebuilding. First, we can try to rebuild the temple as it was. Shirley responded with that kind of determination. She had always wanted to be a mother, but a career delayed her decision to marry and become pregnant.

So her joy was all the more full when she told her husband they were expecting. The pregnancy had its share of problems, but Shirley's spirits were high when labor pains began. But something went dreadfully wrong during the delivery, and the baby boy died. Shirley lamented—and couldn't accept—that she'd never held her son.

Every day, Shirley drove to the hospital and parked out front. She stared at the window of the maternity room, replaying the scene in her mind with a different ending. In her fantasy, as a red-faced, sweet, wailing baby was placed in her arms, she and her husband beamed with happiness.

Shirley resisted her temple's collapse in the most profound way: She denied it. She tried to rebuild her temple, stone by stone, just as it was in her dreams. But when a temple collapses, it can never be reconstructed as it was before.

Passivity. Another way we may respond to a collapsed temple is with passivity. The temple collapses, and we stand before the rubble, expressionless, feeling dead inside. There is no will to move on.

Grace didn't know when the idea formed in her mind; it probably had crept in slowly, unnoticed at first. But with an awful certainty, Grace knew her husband, Bill, was having an affair. Soon she was immersed in divorce proceedings.

Grace and Bill never talked about the affair or the dissolution of their marriage. They discussed the settlement. That is, Bill discussed it, and Grace listened. *What did it matter?* she thought. *Life was over anyway.* Her temple had collapsed, and she stood inert before it.

Standing firm. The best response after a temple collapses is to stand firm with God and work to gain from the experience. When we stand firm, we realize the temple can never look the same, but resources are available to build something new. We know it will take courage, perseverance, and pain to rebuild, but the new construction will hold value and beauty.

I had tried the other two methods of dealing with collapses—rebuilding and passivity—and I knew they didn't work very well. Then a situation taught me how right, and how hard, it is to stand firm.

At work, my supervisor and I had a strained relationship, but I never thought he'd physically attack me. But one day, in a fit of anger, he did.

I wasn't harmed, but I decided to report the incident. In the past, I had accepted much of his abusive behavior, but this situation forced me to realize passivity didn't work. And I knew I couldn't reconstruct the relationship as it existed before, because he had eroded my trust.

But my supervisor did some constructing of his own. He concocted a story that portrayed him as a good-humored fellow and me as an uptight woman who misinterpreted his action. I thought top management might fire me—if they believed my supervisor. One temple had collapsed: my sense of physical well-being. Another was threatened: my economic security.

I painfully labored through that experience: going to work even though I didn't know what would happen; standing firm when called on to retell the incident; crying more than I thought possible.

For four months, the investigation continued. Finally, my supervisor left the company. I never knew if he was fired or if he volunteered to leave.

I'm still rebuilding myself, using the insights and strength I've gained from standing firm when I thought I'd topple. I still need to find grace and forgiveness for those who hurt me, but I believe I will.

When a temple collapses, it usually takes an extended time to recover.

WHERE IS GOD?

Where is God when a temple falls, creating dust clouds and rubble heaps in one great groan? A collapsing temple puts a severe strain on us—it can kill our faith more quickly than any intellectual attack can. And in each of our lives, temples will fall.

Christian Herald magazine conducted a survey that found 13 percent of its subscribers quit reading the Bible because of unanswered prayer.[1] We put a lot of stock in God's responsiveness to us. If He doesn't answer, we may quit relating to Him.

We don't know where God is when we need Him, but we feel sure of one thing: He isn't home for us. We wish He had left His answering machine on so we at least knew our prayers had arrived safely.

But surprisingly, God isn't off attending more urgent matters. In reality, He dwells in the folds of silence that we scorn.

When I hear the fateful rumble of a collapsing temple in my life, followed by an awful silence from God, I picture myself wearing a garment of pain. And I try to envision God lodging in the shadowy folds of that garment. Job 26:14 says, "These are but the outer fringe of his works; how faint the whisper we hear of him! Who then can understand the thunder of his power?"

In recent years, scientists have learned

that at least twelve dimensions exist; yet humans can experience only four of them.[2] God can be closer to us than any person, hovering next to our side, one millimeter from touching us. But we aren't aware of His presence unless He chooses for us to be.

MEMORABLE TRAITS

We can become more aware of God's closeness during our suffering by remembering three characteristics about Him.

Unrushable actions. The first trait to remember about God is that He won't be rushed. Pastor and frequent conference speaker Ron Dunn says much of our praying is trying to get God to hurry up.[3] How much better if we could pray as if we were waiting for the morning.

A psalmist captured this concept in Psalm 130:6-7: "My soul waits for the LORD more than watchmen wait for the morning, more than watchmen wait for the morning. O Israel, put your hope in the LORD, for with the LORD is unfailing love and with him is full redemption."

We know two things about the sun rising: We can't hurry it, and it will come up. The same is true of God. He won't be hurried, but He will show Himself. If we could think of praying as watching God's hand create sunrises in our lives, we wouldn't feel so frustrated when the night seems to drag on.

But I'm more like Debbie, the child of a

friend of mine. One day she announced to her mommy, "I'm sad."

"Why are you sad?" my friend asked.

"Because someone took my way, and I want it back."

So do I, and I tell God often. I must remind myself that sunrises take time, and it's my job to watch, not to create one.

Waiting typically isn't a strong trait of us humans, which may be why God seems to give us ample opportunity to strengthen that quality. Just as a child isn't served well by instant gratification, neither are adults. Patience, insights into ourselves, and space for God to work behind the scenes are all part of the payoff of waiting for the dawn.

Veiled presence. The second characteristic is that God's presence is usually veiled. Few people realize that Michigan has about the same percentage of cloudy days as the Northwest. I lived in Michigan for two years and, from experience, can confirm that statistic.

One day, in the middle of a six-month sunless winter, I sat at my computer, concentrating on my work. Suddenly something outside the window captured my attention. It was a shadow. The sun had shone so little that winter, I'd forgotten shadows existed.

Obviously, the sun does rise in Michigan every day, but when we don't see it, we forget that. It is the same with God's presence in our lives. He is with us, just as the sun shines on a cloudy day. But God's overt appearances are rare—like a bright day in a Michigan winter.

I've been a Christian for twenty-three years. Yet I can count on one hand the times I've felt God's presence: when I became a Christian; when I entered Christian work; when I decided to leave the ministry I'd served with for thirteen years; when my supervisor attacked me. During these times, God deeply touched me.

The only explanation I have for those moments is that the sun emerged from the clouds and revealed itself. And I remember those moments with awe. But usually, God's presence is veiled, and I need to believe, by faith, that He's with me.

This veiling may seem like a strange idea at first for those of us who think of God as up close and personal. Yet, as Job said, we hear only a faint whisper of Him, even though He thunders with power.

God veils Himself because our finite condition can't comprehend infinity. We are like Moses who, when God granted his wish to see God, was only allowed to see His backside. To have viewed God's face would have meant death to Moses. (See Exodus 33:18-23.)

God is simply too big, too powerful, too limitless for us to stand as mortals in His presence. Because of our limits and God's graciousness toward us, we experience Him in veiled ways. It's only at special moments that God grants us the wonder of seeing Him from behind.

Unpredictable ways. The third point regarding God's silence is that He responds in unpredictable ways.

A friend of mine said, "God is utterly faithful and notoriously unpredictable." The story of Lazarus's death confirms this. When Jesus Christ first heard the news of Lazarus's illness, He did the unexpected. He stayed out of town for two more days. Then after He arrived at Lazarus's tomb, He cried.

There is a happy ending to the story: Jesus raised Lazarus from the dead. But He took the unpredictable path to get there— first by delaying, then by weeping. When Jesus saw Lazarus's sister Mary and the Jews weeping over Lazarus's death, He was "deeply moved in spirit and troubled" (John 11:33). His willingness to feel the pain of death, separation from loved ones, and this ultimate price God's created ones must pay for sin, is not something we would have expected from Him.

Ben Patterson, author of the book *Waiting,* told a story that exemplifies God's compassion:

> *I went through two broken engagements over a five-year period—same girl, both times. After the second and final break, I went to visit my friend. I was numb and tired of hurting. I felt dead inside. We talked for a while, and when I got up to leave, he suggested that we pray together.*
>
> *I prayed first, mumbling to God the best theology I could think of under the*

18

*circumstances. I then waited for him to
begin. Nothing came for a long time. I
was about to ask what was wrong when
I heard something—a sob. I asked him
what was wrong. All he could say was,
"It hurts so much."*

"What hurts?" I asked.

*"What's happened to you, stupid!"
he said.*[4]

We often respond as Ben did when
we're hurt. We mumble our way through a
theological dissertation that we call prayer.
Meanwhile, God is there with us.

We could choose to concentrate on
either side of what we see about God in
the story of Lazarus. We could hone in
on His faithfulness and be comforted by
His sharing our pain and taking action
to deal with it. But that would be only
half of who He revealed Himself to be in
that event.

He also took the unpredictable route. If
we forget this element, our ability to remember His faithfulness is shaken. "Why doesn't
He come?" we ask, as we worry over His
delay. And then, when He comes and sits
with us in our season of pain rather than
quickly resolving the problem, we ask, "Why
doesn't He do something?"

But if we can understand that God
expresses both faithfulness and unpredict-
ability, then when He is slow to come, we
can recall that He is faithful. And when He
is slow to heal the pain, we can remember

He is right there with us before He stretches out His hand of healing.

GOD IS THERE

It requires faith to believe that God is hearing our prayers, that He's like the sunrise and won't be hurried to act. It requires faith to believe He's with us, though not in recognizable ways, like the sun on a cloudy day in Michigan. It requires faith to believe that despite His unpredictable ways, He's aching for us, even when we can't cry for ourselves.

But these truths are borne out in our lives more often than our commonly held expectations of prayer: that when we pray God will answer immediately; that He will reveal Himself clearly; that He will fulfill our requests almost precisely.

To continue to hold on to these fallacies can ultimately lead to disillusionment with God and the loss of faith altogether. However, to place our faith in a God who is faithful but slow to act, veiled in our presence, and full of surprises is to encounter a God capable of doing much more than we ever dreamed—in the most satisfying and creative ways.

It's rather like the difference between providing step-by-step directions on preparing a meal to the well-known hostess Martha Stewart or simply showing her where the kitchen is and letting her do whatever her creative juices suggest. With restrictions, Martha wouldn't seem like such a great cook and hostess; one would begin to wonder why everyone makes such a fuss over her. But give her the freedom to express herself, and she'll amaze you.

So, too, our rigid rules and shallow expectations may lead us to abandon prayer. If we could understand how deeply God cares for us in the folds of silence, we would pray as though waiting patiently for the sun to rise. We could rest in God as a temple collapses rather than resist its demise. Being aware of God's presence would console us, even as we feel the pain.

One Palm Sunday, my pastor shared a story that vividly reminded me of God's compassionate presence. He said that two Jewish men had been arrested by the Nazis, then placed in a room with a young boy. German soldiers entered the room and hanged the Jewish boy in front of the men.

But the boy didn't weigh enough to die quickly. It took thirty agonizing minutes for life to choke out of him.

As these two men watched and listened to the boy's agony, one of them asked the other, "Where is God now?"

"Right here," the man answered.

When we suffer, where is our silent God? In the folds of silence. With us. ∎

NOTES
1. "Personal Devotions Live On," *Christian Herald*, January 1988, page 31.
2. Hugh Ross, "Eighties' Astronomy Points to God" (Audiotape), 1987.

3. Ron Dunn, from an address given at Arrowhead
   Springs, San Bernardino, California, March 19,
   1979.
4. Ben Patterson, *Waiting* (Downers Grove, IL: InterVarsity
   Press, 1989), pages 43-44.

Lose Your Security Lately?

*Assess how you respond
to a painful crisis.*

You carry weights in your mind and heart
today—so do most people you encounter.
While all weights are burdensome, each of
us responds to difficulties in individual ways.
Over the years, we've formed our responses
to help us survive.

One necessary part of addressing
God's disturbing silence is to examine your
responses to problems. The questions on
the following pages will help you evaluate
if your responses are more conducive to
finding God or to developing anger and
bitterness.

You may be tempted to give responses
that seem "right" and "spiritual," but ultimately being less than honest hinders you
from finding peace. So take a deep breath
and plunge in.

1. Write a prayer, asking God to help you see yourself honestly, with love rather than condemnation. Ask Him for insights into who you are and how you can relate better to Him.

2. Write down three incidents (including at least one current one) when a temple collapsed in your life. Remember, the temples in our lives can be loved ones, marriage, children, economic support, or physical well-being.

3. As you recall each incident, evaluate how you responded. Then using the list below, write the letter of the response by each incident in question 2.

a. *Rebuilding.* I tried to rebuild this temple. I couldn't accept its collapse and kept replaying the incident with a different ending.

b. *Passivity.* I lost the ability to take action when my temple collapsed. I became passive, neither resisting the collapse nor attempting to move on.

c. *Standing firm.* I stood firm with God and worked to grow from the experience. I knew the temple would never be rebuilt like it was before, but with God's help, I determined to build something new.

4. a. Circle the words that best describe your response to the recent collapse of a temple. Add any others that apply.

sad	passive
bitter	resistant
angry	self-pitying
inactive	close to God
peaceful	far from God
depressed	manipulative of God
accepting	manipulative of others

b. Why did you respond this way to
   the crisis?

5. If your response to a collapsed temple
   could be any color, what color would you
   choose? Why?

6. Write a prayer, asking God to show you
   how to deal with any hindrances from
   experiencing that color. ∎

Expect the Unexpected

*God's ways may puzzle
and surprise you.*

*God is infinite and incomprehensible
and all that is comprehensible about
Him is His infinity and incomprehen-
sibility.* —John of Damascus, eighth-
century church father[1]

One of the most difficult and faith-stretching
aspects of pain is the unexpected and incomprehensible ways of God. You're not alone if
you find God downright puzzling.

Joseph's life is a good example of how
God can be full of surprises. Joseph set his
escapade into motion by flaunting the multi-
hued coat his father had made for him in
front of his brothers. (See Genesis 37:1-11.)
Then his life became a vortex of surprises.
Sold into slavery by his revengeful brothers, Joseph later rose to a peak position as
business manager to one of the Egyptian

Pharaoh's officials. But eventually Joseph hit the pits—literally. He was thrown into prison.

UNDESERVING PAIN

1. Read Genesis 39:2-20. What does this passage say about why we sometimes suffer? List at least three reasons.

2. a. Based on this passage, what can be the results of doing the right thing?

   b. Why does this happen?

28

3. a. Pretend you are in Joseph's situation.
Write to a friend about prison—the
food, your bed, the smells.

   b. What do you miss that you had before
   your personal crisis hit?

4. a. Read Genesis 39:21-23. How did God
   act on Joseph's behalf?

b. What didn't God do for Joseph?

5. What do these verses teach you about
   God's ways during suffering?

RELEASED AT LAST

More than two years passed before Joseph
left prison. His release was unforeseeable, so
was the position he attained. Joseph became
prime minister of Egypt. (See Genesis
41:14-41.)

Joseph prepared the land to sustain
seven years of famine by filling huge grana-
ries. In the midst of the famine, his brothers
approached him to buy food. They didn't
recognize this powerful, bewigged Egyptian
as the little brother who presumably died
long ago. (See Genesis 42:1-6.)

6. In Genesis 42–44, Joseph recognized his brothers and wept, but he didn't reveal his identity. Read these chapters quickly. Why do you think Joseph put his brothers through this set of circumstances?

7. Read Genesis 45:1-9.

   a. Why do you think Joseph finally revealed his identity?

   b. Why do you think he wept?

c. What other ways could Joseph have responded?

8. What attitudes sustained Joseph through suffering and guided his decision to help his brothers?

9. When do you think Joseph first realized God's purposes behind his suffering?

10. Contrast this encounter with Joseph's relationship to his brothers before they sold him (Genesis 37:5-8). How did suffering change Joseph?

11. What could have happened if Joseph had gained power over his brothers without the interim suffering?

12. How could suffering be changing you?

TWICE FRUITFUL

Reading an overview of Joseph's life, it's easy to see God's hand. But imagine how mysterious—and awful—the events were for Joseph as they unfolded.

Even though this story had a happy ending, Joseph didn't forget his suffering. He named his second child Ephraim, which means "twice fruitful." Joseph explained: "God has made me fruitful in the land of my suffering" (Genesis 41:52). He never considered Egypt home; it was a place of pain.

13. List everything you can think of that Joseph lost because of his suffering. Then list everything he gained.

LOST	GAINED

14. What does Joseph's life teach you about God's ways?

15. a. List the events in your life that cause pain and seem without reason. Then list what you might lose and gain from each event.

34

EVENT	LOSSES/GAINS

b. How do you feel about these losses
   and gains?

This week, pray through the lists in question 15, explaining to God how you feel about each item. Ask God to help you trust Him and to make this painful time fruitful, even though you cannot imagine good results.

Then begin a chart to track the good things that happen during the next month. Remember, good things can seem small when you're hurting. Record them anyway.

And sometimes good things can be the realization of our weakness and need for God, understanding unpleasant aspects of ourselves, and so on. Then thank God for each expression of His love during your pain. ∎

NOTE
1. Elisabeth Elliot, *Let Me Be a Woman* (Wheaton, IL: Tyndale House, 1976), page 20.

Of Guarantees and Warranties

*God doesn't promise
to always rescue you.*

An anguished mother wrote to a friend of the death of her twenty-three-year-old daughter:

> *God, who could have helped, looked
> down on a young woman devoted to Him,
> quite willing to die for Him to give Him
> glory, and decided to sit on His hands
> and let her death top the horror charts
> for [cystic fibrosis] deaths.*[1]

Why does God allow the senseless suffering of good people? Through the ages, this question has perplexed Christians.

HALL OF FAITH

Hebrews 11 has been called the "Hall of Faith." Reading this chapter is like strolling through a museum commemorating those who acted bravely and gloriously for God.

Often we think faith came naturally for these people. But was it really that easy?

1. a. According to Hebrews 11:1-3, what is faith?

   b. According to these verses, why do we need faith?

2. Now read verses 4-31. List some of the people who followed God "by faith," along with their actions and rewards.

PERSON/ACTION	REWARD

3. According to verses 13-16, what made these people faith-filled and commended by God?

4. Read Hebrews 11:32-35a. What are the results of faith?

TWO EXTREMES

5. Read Hebrews 11:35b-40. Do these verses change your answer to question 4? If so, how?

6. Compare the first half of verse 35 with the last half. What do these two extremes reveal about suffering and God's answers to prayer?

7. a. What might have stimulated the Hebrews 11 people's willingness to suffer?

   b. What did they share in common?

8. According to verse 40, what is the ultimate goal of our faith? (The word *perfect* means "fulfilled" or "finished."[2])

9. Hebrews 12:1. How do the "Hall of Faith-ers" affect your life today?

10. a. In Hebrews 12:2-3, Jesus Christ is called the "author and perfecter of our faith." How did He earn this distinction?

    b. How can Christ's example encour-age you?

11. Verses 4-11 suggest another reason God may allow us to feel pain. Summarize that reason and describe how this explanation makes you feel.

12. a. From what you've learned so far, what are possible reasons God may allow you to suffer when it's "not your fault"?

    b. Do these reasons help you accept the suffering? Explain.

Jesus Christ is our example of someone who was faith-filled, yet God the Father allowed Him to suffer and die. Read about these events in Matthew 27:32–28:5.

13. According to the following verses, why was Christ allowed to suffer?

   Romans 5:6-8

   Romans 6:3-4

   John 14:1-3

14. Below are concentric circles representing the weekend when Christ died and later rose from the dead.

   a. In the circle labeled "Good Friday," list what was lost when Christ died on the cross.

   b. In the outermost circle, "Easter Sunday," list what was gained on that day.

   c. In the middle circle, "Saturday," describe how Christ's followers must have felt on this day.

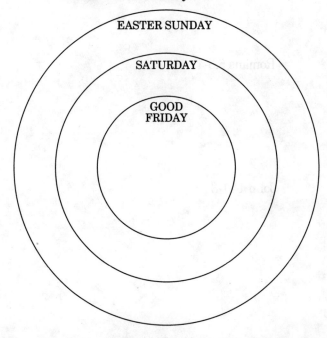

EASTER SUNDAY

SATURDAY

GOOD
FRIDAY

44

15. Now draw three similar circles to represent the seasons you will experience as you suffer.

    a. In the inner circle, list what you have lost.

    b. In the middle circle, list how you feel while suffering.

    c. In the outer circle, list the new things you hope for as a result of suffering.

HOPE AND HELP

16. According to the following verses, what hope do we have as we live through our own "Dark Saturdays"?

Psalm 7:19-20

Romans 5:3-5

Ephesians 3:16-19

Titus 1:2

17. What help is available to us when we are not able to see any reason for our suffering?

John 14:26

Romans 15:4

Hebrews 10:23-25

FINDING FAITH

This week, use a concordance to locate and write out Bible verses that define and describe faith. Then answer the following questions:

- What is the evidence of faith?

- How do I obtain faith?

- How can faith affect how I live?

- How does God view faith?

- Do I live by faith?

- How can I become a more faith-filled person? ■

NOTES
1. Philip Yancey, *Disappointment With God* (Grand Rapids, MI: Zondervan Publishing, 1988), page 158.
2. William F. Arndt and F. Wilbur Gingrich (translators and adaptors), *A Greek-English Lexicon of the New Testament and Other Early Christian Literature* (Chicago: University of Chicago Press, 1979), page 809.

Lookin' Good Ain't Enough

*Develop a healthy heart
in a sick situation.*

Stars, not scars. Better or bitter? These
phrases, along with a reminder that "all
things work together for good" (Romans 8:28)
often are offered by well-meaning Christians when you're in physical or emotional
pain. They're given as reminders that you
have choices about your attitudes while
suffering.

Even though the intentions are good,
these phrases can sound like worn-out
clichés. Other people's expectations can
induce you to pretend as though you're
handling pressure points with grace and
spirituality.

But looking good doesn't matter to
God. He wants your heart and soul to be
healthy. He wants you to become more
and more like Jesus in your response to
pain.

49

1. God spells out the characteristics of a
   healthy heart in Micah 6:8. First, write
   out the three things He requires of us.
   Then describe what you think each
   phrase means.

2. a. In front of each incident below, write
      the letter(s) that correspond(s) with
      the heart qualities that would be hard
      to express in these times of suffering.

      KEY: A=act justly; B=love mercy;
           C=walk humbly with God.

      _C_ Wrongfully fired

      _B_ Husband unfaithful

      _A_ Robbed of valuables

_B_ Lied to by best friend

_B_ Father died of a heart attack

_C_ Cheated by business associate

_AB_ Child killed by drunken driver

_C_ Insurance company won't pay

_B_ Church member spreads an
   untrue rumor about you

b. Place an asterisk by each item that
   went wrong because of a relationship.
   How can suffering and relationships
   be tied together?

   *Our suffering is often caused
   by our relationship*

3. How could the qualities of a healthy
   heart balance each other when you're
   tempted to act in the following ways?

   Feel superior:

51

Be vindictive:

Win, regardless of the cost:

Let someone take advantage of you:

CHAIN OF RESPONSES

Isaac was unwittingly placed in a situation
that demanded a healthy heart. Although

he was living in the land God promised him, it was ruled by the Philistines. Isaac was a mere sojourner.

4. Look up Genesis 26:12-31. Write in each chain-link the event that Isaac experienced.

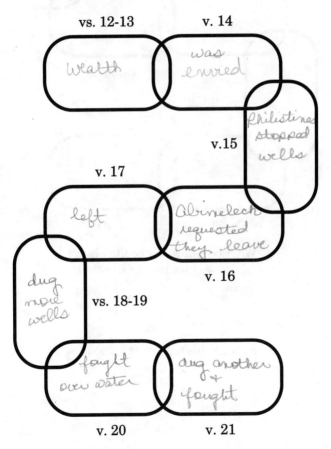

vs. 12-13 — Wealth

v. 14 — was envied

v.15 — Philistines stopped wells

v. 17 — left

v. 16 — Abimelech requested they leave

vs. 18-19 — dug more wells

v. 20 — fought over water

v. 21 — dug another + fought

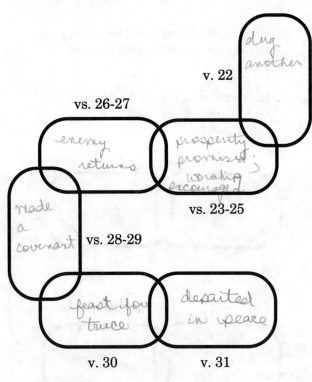

v. 22
dug
another

vs. 26-27
enemy
returns

vs. 23-25
prosperity
promised;
worship
encouraged

vs. 28-29
made
a
covenant

v. 30
feast for
truce

v. 31
departed
in peace

5. a. What qualities of a healthy heart
did Isaac show throughout these
events?

   b. How did his neighbors respond
to him?

c. What was God's response to him?

6. Draw a chain of events in a strained relationship that contributes to your suffering.

7. In the situation outlined in question 6, how can you respond according to Micah 6:8? Complete the following sentences.

I can act justly by . . .

I can love mercy by . . .

I can walk humbly with God by . . .

8. What personal adjustments will be necessary to respond in the ways you described in question 7?

PAINFUL PERSEVERANCE

9. How did the following biblical characters persevere during painful times?

Esther (Esther 4:9-16)

David (Psalm 138)

Daniel (Daniel 6:6-23)

Belief in God by Daniel & Darius

Father of demon-possessed man (Mark 9:17-24)

10. How can you apply the responses of the people in question 9 to your crisis? (What example have they set for you?)

Praise, Belief + Prayer

11. a. What can you do to persevere through
       a current crisis? List three things.

    b. What heart attitudes and responses
       are you willing to express? List at
       least three.

FINDING COMFORT

Developing godly heart qualities during a
crisis is hard work. But God is with us and
comforts us throughout trials.

    This week, choose a godly heart quality
and, each day, keep a journal of how you
work to infuse it into your relationships.
Write about the difficulties and triumphs,
then share your experiences with a trusted
friend. ■

Who Me, Mad?

*When God does something
you don't like.*

When I'm under stress, I lock myself out of
the house. I don't mean to; it just happens
because I'm busy thinking about problems.
One week this year, I locked myself out
four times.

Every time I discovered myself on the
outside looking in, I asked, "God, how could
You do this to me?" The question betrayed
my misaligned thought processes. Why would
I blame God for my mental preoccupation?

My second response was to pray for
a quick and inexpensive way out of the
problem.

My third response was to pray one of my
neighbors was home.

If God failed to answer my prayers, I
became intensely angry with His lack of
cooperation. It's true: My response was silly
and immature. But when hard times encamp

around us, we don't always react nobly.

One book of the Bible centers on a man who is a caricature of every bad response I've ever had. He would have lambasted God for locking him out of the house, too. But before we take a look at him, how about an inventory of your own?

TAKING STOCK

Psychologists tell us anger is a part of suffering. Elisabeth Kubler-Ross, famous for her work on the psychological effects of facing death, lists anger as a key phase in a healthy response to grief.[1]

But sometimes anger gets misdirected. Take a few minutes to examine your response to a latest crisis.

1. When your crisis hit, what was your first thought?

2. a. What did you ask God to do?

b. How long did you remain in the situation before you prayed?

c. What was your response if God didn't answer in the way you asked?

3. On a scale of "1" to "10," with "10" as the greatest amount, how angry were you with God? ___ How angry are you now? ___ How disappointed? ___

JONAH'S PROBLEMS

If your response to God was less than you'd hoped, Jonah's story should encourage you. He seemed to experience a chronic pout. To overview how he interacted with God, read the book of Jonah in one sitting. (It'll only take a few minutes.)

4. On the following chart, list Jonah's problems, his response to each problem, and God's response to Jonah.

JONAH'S PROBLEMS & RESPONSES	GOD'S RESPONSES
1. Go to Ninevah - fled	- chased w/ wind
* 2. storm cast into sea	- storm ceased sent whale
*3. swallowed by whale - prayed	- whale spit him out
4. Go to Ninevah - went preaching	- God saved & spared city
5. God spared Ninevah - angry; sat & pouted	- God grew a gourd & made a worm eat it
*6. heat, fainted "better to die	-

5. a. Review the chart and put an asterisk by each problem Jonah created for himself. Below, list Jonah's actions or attitudes that caused his problems.

unwillingness to obey God

selfishness

anger

b. Did Jonah's anger compound his problems? Explain.

Because of his anger chap. 4 he could not understand God's mercy so he sat & pouted till he fainted from the heat.

6. a. What was bad about the way Jonah viewed God?

He saw Him as a Judge only without mercy + compassion salvation

b. How did this view cause him greater difficulties?

Caused God to show Jonah he was both

7. a. What was good about the way Jonah viewed God?

Chapter 2
He knew sin separated him from God but God would forgive

b. How did it help him in his circumstances?

Helped him get out of belly of whale

8. In what ways are your responses to a crisis similar to Jonah's? In what ways are they dissimilar?

SIMILAR	DISSIMILAR

9. a. If you feel angry, how is this response destructive in your situation?

b. How can your anger be constructive in this situation?

10. a. What weaknesses did Jonah display more than once in his journey?

Disobedience
angered easily

b. What strengths did he show?

Acknowledged he was wrong

c. How did God display a knowledge of both Jonah's frailty and sturdiness?

65

11. a. As you look over past crises in your life, what recurring weaknesses do you see?

b. What strengths?

c. How did God display a knowledge of both your frailty and your sturdiness?

d. What aspects of your response to a crisis might you change to avoid future catastrophes?

12. Based on Jonah's story, how does God want us to respond when we discover we're at least partly responsible for our problems?

humility   repentance

13. a. In what ways are you responsible for your latest crisis?

b. How can you take responsibility for your actions?

14. Which of God's responses to your crisis, on the surface, seem maddening?

PLAUSIBLE ENDINGS

15. How did Jonah's attitudes, expressed in his prayer in chapter 2, differ from the attitudes he expressed in most of the book?

16. Do you think Jonah was repentant?

    a. Defend your position based on Jonah's prayer.

       Sorry he was caught
       no care

b. Defend your position based on Jonah's behavior in chapter 4.

17. a. Do you need to repent of any attitudes or actions that might contribute to your present crisis? Explain.

b. What can you learn from Jonah that will help you show your sincerity to God?

18. God left the story of Jonah unfinished. Write an ending to this story, based on how you think Jonah responded.

19. Write an ending to your own crisis—the way you'd like to respond.

DIGGING OUT ANGER

This week, write out your answers to the following questions:

- In regard to my current crisis, what am I angry about?

- Am I angry at God because of this crisis? Why, or why not?

- Should I hide my anger from God? Explain.

- How might God respond if I honestly admit my anger to Him?

- What will happen if I harbor anger?

Based on your answers, admit your anger to God. Then ask Him to lead you to forgiveness: from Him for your sins; for yourself for your failings; for others for how they've hurt you. ∎

NOTE
1. Elisabeth Kubler-Ross, *On Death and Dying* (New York: Macmillan Publishing Co., 1969), page 50.

The Quintessential Sufferer

Job's example can help you find rest.

No study on suffering could be complete without discussing Job, the quintessential sufferer. He asked all the "why" questions that burn on our lips.

All of Job's "temples" fell down at once—his possessions were destroyed or stolen; his children were killed; his friends turned on him; his wife emotionally deserted him; his body collapsed in pain. Few of us will know the suffering Job experienced. (See Job 1:13-18, 2:7.)

BOOK OF QUESTIONS

Probably no other book in the Bible asks more questions than Job. In its pages, Job's wife questioned why he didn't curse God and die. Job questioned God regarding his suffering. Job's friends questioned him regarding

sin that might have caused the suffering.
(You may want to read the book, noting the
questions asked.)

Finally, in the last chapters of Job, God
responded—with questions.

1. In your own words, write the beginning
   of God's response to Job in 38:2-7.

2. a. How do you think Job felt at this
      point?

b. Why do you think God responded with these questions?

GOD OF THE UNIVERSE

God's discourse continued, listing ways He expresses control over His universe. (To appreciate God's power, read Job 38:8–39:30.)

In 40:2, God invited Job to argue his case. He demanded, "Let him who accuses God answer him!"

3. a. Read Job's response in 40:4-5. Write the response in your own words.

b. Why do you think Job responded
   this way?

4. God answered with more challenges to
   Job in 40:6–41:34. Summarize what God
   taught Job through this response.

5. a. Read Job's response in 42:1-6. What
      did he finally understand about God?

b. What did Job mean by, "My ears had
   heard of you but now my eyes have
   seen you"?

c. Why do you think Job repented?

REST AT LAST

6. Through His questions and answers,
   God led Job over steppingstones to
   find faith and rest. From the following passages, list the steps God led Job
   through.

   Job 38:2-7

Job 40:2

Job 40:4-5

Job 40:6–41:34

Job 42:1-6

7. Write the questions you are burning to ask God about your crisis. What questions might He ask you in reply to each concern?

Your question:

God's question:

Your question:

God's question:

Your question:

God's question:

8. What steppingstones might God need to lead you through?

9. What message from God would help you find rest in your crisis?

BACKGROUND EVENTS

When Job accepted God's response and repented, he did not know about the behind-the-scene events that initiated his calamities.

10. a. Read Job 1:12 and 2:1-6. Why did God allow Satan to inflict pain on Job?

   b. Do you think Satan is always the instigator of our suffering? Why, or why not?

11. a. What does Job's prayer in Job 1:21 teach us about a God-honoring way to respond to calamity?

b. What makes it difficult to maintain that attitude? Consider events, attitudes, people's comments or actions, spiritual warfare.

c. Which of the elements in question 11b might affect answers to prayer?

HANGING ON

While this study has focused on God's silent times, we must not forget that God *really does* answer prayer and works all things together for good (Romans 8:28).

12. a. Read Job 42:10-16. How did God restore Job's life?

b. Which of the following do you think is true?

- Job viewed God as having made a lame attempt to replace his children and material possessions.

- Job was filled with gratitude for his second start in life.

- Job had mixed emotions about what God had done in restoring his life.

c. What do you think Job said to God as he surveyed the ways He had restored his life?

d. What attitudes would cause Job to respond that way?

13. From what you've read in this lesson, how much of this restoration was dependent on God's actions? On Job's?

14. What do the following passages teach about persevering through pain?

Psalm 30:5

2 Corinthians 1:3-4

Hebrews 4:15-16

Romans 8:35-39

16. From what you've learned in this study, complete the following statements.

Even though I don't understand the "why" of my suffering, I can respond by . . .

God may be allowing this pain to make these changes in me . . .

While I'm suffering, I can count on God to . . .

If God answers my prayers, I want my attitude to be . . .

If God does not answer my prayers, I
want my attitude to be . . .

If my crisis isn't resolved the way I
want, God may still "work things for
good" by . . .

MY COMMITMENT

17. Read Matthew 22:37-38 and consider the
    following quote:

    *To be commanded to love God at all, let
    alone in the wilderness, is like being com-
    manded to be well when we are sick, to
    sing for joy when we are dying of thirst, to
    run when our legs are broken.*
    *But this is the first and great com-
    mandment nonetheless. Even in the
    wilderness—especially in the wilder-
    ness—you shall love Him.*[1]

84

a. How willing are you to love God in the wilderness?

b. How can you commit yourself to loving Him?

A REMINDER

These five lessons are not the final word on understanding how we relate to God as we suffer. The final word has not yet been spoken and won't be until Christ returns, makes all things new, and eradicates suffering (Revelation 21:1-4).

While we each gain something from suffering, it still hurts. And we'll never fully know what it was about because God's ways are often swathed in shadows.

If we can become more aware of His presence while we suffer, then our questions have their own reward, just as Job's did. ∎

NOTE
1. Frederick Buechner, *A Room Called Remember* (San Francisco, CA: Harper & Row, 1984), page 41.

DIALOGUE

Making Sense of Suffering

*Questions for group
or individual reflection.*

WHEN GOD SEEMS SO SILENT

1. Do you know someone who lost his or her faith because of suffering? What was it about the suffering that caused a loss of faith? (Do not mention names.)
2. Who do you know who grew stronger in their faith because of suffering? What attitudes caused this growth in faith?
3. Why is it difficult to accept that God will not be rushed? That His presence is usually veiled? That His ways are surprising?
4. What is the most difficult aspect of God's silence?
5. Recount a time you prayed for something and it eventually happened. What were the special surprises in how God answered your prayer?

6. When we suffer, why do we struggle to believe God is compassionate?

LESSON ONE

1. Which temples collapsed for Jesus during His life? (Temples are loved ones, marriage, children, economic support, physical well-being.) If you need help, look at these verses: Matthew 8:20, 12:46-50, 27:26-31.
2. In what ways could Jesus' knowledge of His death be akin to the suffering during a terminal illness? See Mark 8:31.
3. How did Jesus respond to His suffering in Luke 4:1-41 and 22:42? What emotions did He feel? What helped Him to stand firm?
4. Read Isaiah 53:2-9, a prophecy regarding Jesus' life. In a sense, it is His obituary, written hundreds of years before His birth. In what additional ways did Jesus suffer?
5. What does Matthew 25:34-40 say about God's identification with those who suffer?
6. How can Christ's suffering comfort our pain?

LESSON TWO

1. Hebrews 12:2 says Jesus chose to suffer and die. How can this fact change our view of the pain He endured?
2. Does this mean we should passively accept suffering? Why, or why not?
3. According to Philippians 2:5-11, what did

Jesus gain because of His willingness to
suffer? What did we gain because of His
suffering?
4. What might we gain because of our suffering? What might we lose? Which of
these items are temporal and which are
eternal?
5. How can we develop an eternal view of
our suffering?
6. What relief would we like from our suffering right now?

LESSON THREE

1. What does Ecclesiastes 3:1-8 tell us
about suffering? Does this make us hope-
ful or sad?
2. Theologian Nathan Koller says the
more radical the suffering, the more
probable it is that the resulting change
will be radical.[1] How was this true in
Jesus' death?
3. Based on Koller's statement, what
changes can we expect in our lives
because of our crises?
4. What role does Jesus' resurrection play
in our view of suffering?
5. How does that fit with Ecclesiastes 3:1-8?
6. How can suffering create a resurrection
in our lives?

LESSON FOUR

1. T. S. Eliot describes God as "the still
point of the turning world."[2] How might

this concept help us handle suffering?
2. In what ways does suffering create chaos in our lives?
3. What action does God take against chaos in Genesis 1:2-3? What does He intend to do with chaos?
4. How can we share in God's action?
5. What does God promise He will do regarding the chaos of earth in Revelation 21:1-6? What consolation does that give us today?
6. What do these verses say about God's awareness of our individual sufferings?

LESSON FIVE

1. Read Matthew 28:1-9. When the women went to the tomb, what did they expect to find? In what ways do we enter into a suffering experience like these women?
2. How might the two Marys have responded when they saw what greeted them at the tomb? Which of their emotions are similar to the ones we experience when we're suffering?
3. What hope did the angel give them? How do we hold the same hopes as we suffer?
4. What did the women experience in verses 8-9? How do their experiences correlate to times of suffering?
5. What choices did the women make? In what ways do we have to face the same choices when suffering inflicts us?

6. What is the best choice we can make concerning our current suffering? ■

NOTES
1. Nathan Koller, *Songs of Suffering* (Minneapolis, MN: Winston Press, 1982), page 114.
2. T. S. Eliot, "Burnt Norton," *Chief Modern Poets of Britain and America*, vol. II (New York: Macmillan Publishing Company), page 284.

B I B L I O G R A P H Y

Making More Sense

Suggested readings to console and encourage.

Davis, Ron Lee. *Gold in the Making*. Nashville, TN: Thomas Nelson Publishers, 1983.

Emerson, James G. *Suffering: Its Meaning and Ministry*. Nashville, TN: Abingdon Press, 1986.

Frankl, Viktor E. *Man's Search for Meaning*. New York: Simon and Schuster, 1970.

Kollar, Nathan. *Songs of Suffering*. Minneapolis, MN: Winston Press, 1982.

Kreeft, Peter. *Making Sense of Suffering*. Ann Arbor, MI: Servant Books, 1986.

Kubler-Ross, Elisabeth. *On Death and Dying*. New York: Macmillan Publishing Company, 1969.

Lewis, C. S. *A Grief Observed.* New York: Bantam Books, 1963.

Lewis, C. S. *The Problem of Pain.* New York: Macmillan Publishing Company, 1962.

Nouwen, C. S. *The Wounded Healer.* New York: Doubleday & Company, 1979.

Schaeffer, Edith. *Affliction.* Old Tappan, NJ: Fleming H. Revell Company, 1978.

Tournier, Paul. *Creative Suffering.* San Francisco, CA: Harper & Row, 1981.

Yancey, Philip. *Disappointment With God.* Grand Rapids, MI: Zondervan Publishing House, 1988. ∎

A U T H O R

Janet Kobobel is managing editor of books for Focus on the Family. She has also worked as an editor for the publications department of Campus Crusade for Christ and for several other Christian organizations. In addition to writing, she spends her free time adding to her cookbook collection and sometimes even cooking. ■

OTHER TITLES IN THIS SERIES

Additional *CRISISPOINTS* Bible studies include:

Getting a Grip on Guilt by Judith Couchman. Learn to live a life free from guilt.

Nobody's Perfect, So Why Do I Try to Be? by Nancy Groom. Get over the need to do everything right.

So What If You've Failed? by Penelope J. Stokes. Use your mistakes to become a more loving, godly woman.

When You Can't Get Along by Gloria Chisholm. How to resolve conflict according to the Bible.

When Your Marriage Disappoints You by Janet Chester Bly. Hope and help for improving your marriage.

Why Is Her Life Better Than Mine? by Judith Couchman. How to confront jealousy, comparison, and competition.

You're Better Than You Think! by Madalene Harris. How to overcome shame and develop a healthy self-image.

These studies can be purchased at a Christian bookstore. Or order a catalog from NavPress, Customer Services, P. O. Box 35001, Colorado Springs, CO 80935. Or call 1-800-366-7788 for information. ∎